TO
Mike

Michael
McKinley

TAKE CARE OF YOUR BUSINESS...

or Someone Else Will

Michael McKinley, CSP, CPAE

Library of Congress Cataloging-in-Publication Data
McKinley, Michael
    Take care of your business—or someone else will / Michael McKinley.
        p.   cm.
        ISBN 1-888222-09-3 (hardcover)
        1. Customer services.   2. Signs and signboards.   I. Title.
HF5415.5.M4   1997   97-35855
658--dc21   CIP

Printed in the United States of America

Cover Design by Kris Madsen

**THINKING
PUBLICATIONS**®
A Division of McKinley Companies, Inc.

424 Galloway Street
Eau Claire, WI 54703
(800) 225-GROW • FAX (800) 828-8885
E-mail: custserv@ThinkingPublications.com
www.AliveAlive.com

DEDICATION

To Nancy, who believed in me before I believed in me;

To Paul and Gladys, the reason I am here; and

To Kevin, Mary, and Christopher,
who continue to teach me how to be a parent

TABLE OF CONTENTS

CHAPTER 1

CUSTOMERS—
THE REASON
BUSINESS EXISTS

found this in a back hallway where all the employees of a hotel congregate. It really is a complete mission statement. Any customer would feel good if the people who served them took care of these three things. Business really is simple, isn't it?

INSIGHT #1

Know your
mission at work.

T his sign was by the front door of a restaurant. Most of the time when you go into a restaurant, they command you to be seated and you have to wait. Not here. This was a great restaurant. They not only greeted us but they allowed us to choose the place where we wanted to sit. The chef even came out and introduced himself, then asked if there was anything special that we wanted. I was frightened. I knew the meal was going to cost a lot of money. I was right, and I happily paid the money.

Provide
special service
and customers
will feel good about
paying more...
then coming back again.

A long with appreciation, customers are interested in convenience and speed. This "Inconvenience Store" provided neither. Notice the front door. It seems like it has been beaten down a few times. Was that from people trying to get in...or out?

INSIGHT #3

If you forgo
convenience,
customers
won't feel good
about paying more.

This is a great quote from Jay Leno. How many times do we not get thanked properly? Some businesses are notorious for failing to thank customers. Wouldn't you be shocked to have someone standing at the front door of those businesses saying thank you? At each one, you'd be thinking, "This place is going under! I know it!" If that's our reaction, it means we aren't getting thanked enough!

When I chided a supermarket clerk for failing to say thank you, she snapped, "It's printed on your receipt!"

Jay Leno

INSIGHT #4

Focus on
appreciation,
the backbone of
customer loyalty.

Businesses walk a fine line between being too "pushy" and not pushy enough. How many times as a customer have you wanted something but no one would wait on you? Many people have gone out of business because they forgot to ask their customers if they wanted to buy. Some businesses have viewed customers as the enemy— people who just walked through with no intent to buy.

INSIGHT #5

Believe people
will buy,
ask them,
and some will.

G oing in search of a salesperson is *not* something that most of us like to do or have the time to do. We want to be served by someone who's attentive to our needs and helps us fulfill those needs with no hassle attached.

Make it easy
for customers to do
business with you.

You might not want to go in these businesses. In fact, you can't, because the doors are locked! "Weather" they'll open again is anyone's guess.

INSIGHT #7

Consider the relationship
between your business
and the weather from
your customer's perspective.
(Most customers expect
you to provide service
no matter what.)

Several years ago, Holiday Inn had a slogan. What did they mean by "stay with someone you know"? Are they trying to drive business away? I walked up to the counter and asked, "Do you know anyone I could stay with?" They looked at me funny.

"Haircut while you wait." Is there any other way? I don't think anyone is going to say, "Can I just leave my head here and I'll pick it up at 4:00?"

INSIGHT #8

Customers interpret
our signs any way
they want to.

'm not always a logical person but this seems a bit illogical to me. How about the person who painted the sign? How about the person who put up the sign? How about the person who requested that the sign be made? I would really like to see some clean dirt. Perhaps they use some special soap.

Beware that
oxymorons
can be fun—
or confusing—
for your customers.

This is one of my favorite signs. Can you see the anger in the sign? This happened to be on the front door of a candy store. Someone obviously made the workers really angry by coming in and asking for ice cream. Well, I walked around a five- to six-block area to find ice cream, and there was no ice cream anywhere!

I learned something from this sign: If enough people come in and ask for ice cream, maybe we should sell ice cream! (This is what we call "market research"!) By the way, I was with Nancy, my wife, and I begged her, "Please, please, can I go in and ask?" She replied, "No, I can see from the sign they'll probably have a gun and shoot you."

INSIGHT #10

Listen to your customers;
they'll tell you what
you should be selling.

This sign gives a mixed message. A mixed message can create a mixed emotion. Remember the old quip, "A mixed emotion is what you get when your 17-year-old daughter comes up the driveway at 4:00 a.m. with a Gideons Bible under her arm." You don't want your customers feeling like they're the parents of that 17-year-old.

INSIGHT #11

Provide only
positive messages
when people come to
your place of business.

I would suggest you don't call your business "BM Service." I think people would probably question whether they want to come into BM Service. After I had taken the picture of BM Service, I noticed several years later that they must have had a marketing meeting and expanded what they were selling. The new sign? "BM Gas and Service."

INSIGHT #12

Businesses can
attract (or deter)
customers
with their name.

The owner of this hot dog cart was tremendously creative. He listed the entire menu of what he sold on the door of his cart. I can just hear someone saying, "Oh, let's go down to the 'Big Weenie' and have lunch!"

Here's another interesting marketing campaign, this time from a hotel. Maybe I don't understand the meaning, but I think their customers do!

INSIGHT #13

Marketing plans come
in many different
sizes and colors.

Hopefully, the people who run this business don't get these two mixed up for their customers. This is not what I would call a healthy product mix for a store to have. I wonder what else they sell!

He're's another company that should make up its mind what business they're in. When's the last time you've heard, "Yeah, I'd like some of your strawberry yogurt, and give me a large beer to go with that!"

INSIGHT #14

Diversify in a way
that makes sense to your customers.

found this sign in a motel. They don't understand that customers will pay any amount of money to stay in a room if they can get free ice. If for some reason the ice machine can't make enough ice, why not buy a new ice machine? I know people who go out of their way to stay at hotels that say, "Sure! Fill up your coolers!" We're giving away water here, folks! Customers often don't expect much, but when they don't even get their minimal expectations met, they complain and remember for a long time.

INSIGHT #15

Indulge customers
with free "stuff"
whenever you can.

ere are two signs for customers who take free "stuff" when it's not intended to be free. Even so, do you think these messages read a bit strong? You decide.

INSIGHT #16

It's OK to let
your customers
know what's fair
to take for free
and what's not.

found this sign in a store. I love this sign. The owner of this business is having some fun and yet giving the message to customers to keep children under their control.

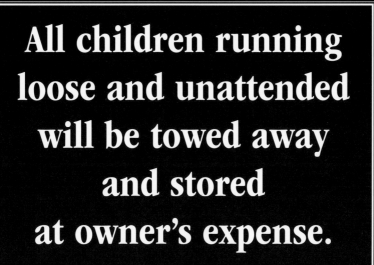

All children running loose and unattended will be towed away and stored at owner's expense.

INSIGHT #17

Let your customers
know what you need
and expect from them.

Have you stood in a checkout lane and watched kids scream and yell as someone is trying to pay for their groceries? This sign was made to help those people. Well, the kids will wise up soon. They'll start screaming and yelling before the checkout lane. Why? You guessed it...to get in the lane with the candy.

For Shoppers With Children:

This Checkout Has No Candy

← This Lane

INSIGHT #18

Do what you can to
make shopping
with children a
pleasant experience;
it will keep the
adults coming back.

C hili's has some fun with their customers about their parking policy. I parked about three blocks away just to make sure that I got my car back.

PARKING
CHILI'S
CUSTOMERS
ONLY
OTHER CARS WILL
BE CRUSHED AND
MELTED

INSIGHT #19

Make spending money
with your business fun!

B eing in business these days is a full-time job and then some! Customers expect us to be available when they're ready to spend their money. And if we're not available, guess what? One of our competitors will be!

INSIGHT #20

Take care of your business...

or someone else will!

CHAPTER 2

TEAMWORK AND LEADERSHIP IN BUSINESS

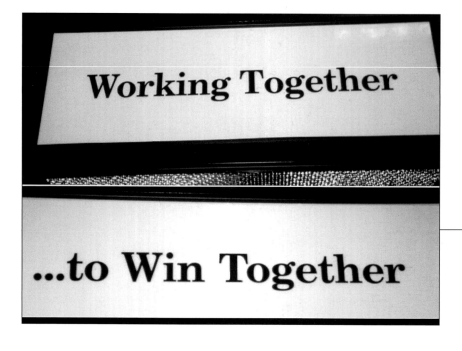

These signs really depict what teamwork is all about. Teams need to have a cooperative partnership of trust, honesty, communication, investigation, and caring. The best teams are people who are working toward a common goal, who know what the goal will do for them and those they serve, and who continue to work together as a team even though they come from diverse backgrounds and have different personalities.

INSIGHT #21

Build strong teams
if you want a
strong organization.

I know that this sign simplifies how we might approach teamwork. I wrote it some time ago and I think it still holds true. Wouldn't you love to work with people who believe in being firm, fair, flexible, and fun? (Wouldn't you love to be married to someone like this?)

B Firm
Fair
Flexible
Fun

INSIGHT #22

If each of us
would individually
commit to being
firm, fair, flexible, and fun,
we'd build incredibly
strong teams at work
(and at home).

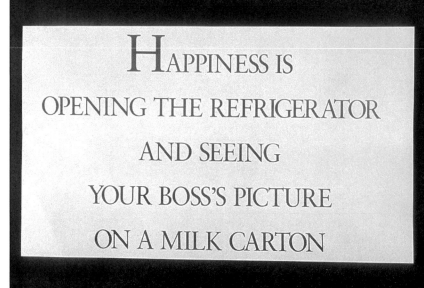

HAPPINESS IS
OPENING THE REFRIGERATOR
AND SEEING
YOUR BOSS'S PICTURE
ON A MILK CARTON

One day on my desk, I got this sign. This certainly would make people want to have a good day, don't you think? Then I was gone about three days, and when I came back, the milk carton on the next page was sitting on my desk!

INSIGHT #23

The "fun" part
of teamwork is
important to model;
be able to
laugh at yourself.

Of course, work can be a real zoo, and we're the wild animals in that zoo! In fact, some days it's actually like Camp He Ho Ha. Some days it's hard to find the difference between sanity and insanity.

INSIGHT #24

Everybody has days
when they say,
"Boy, today was a laugher!"...
and, long-term,
the work still gets done.

B eing from Wisconsin, I thought, "This is a great picture!" We all make mistakes. Hopefully, we learn from those mistakes and move on.

INSIGHT #25

The smartest leaders
and the strongest teams
have often made
the most mistakes
in the past.

These two pictures provide a little leadership seminar. Today's leaders and managers need to be a resource to their people rather than supervisors who chew out people. They need to be part of a team, not put on a pedestal.

INSIGHT #26

Guide people
toward a common goal
and they'll know who
the leader is.

One of the first real jobs that my youngest son had when he was a teenager was working in a medical clinic. He didn't do well in high school, and his self-esteem was sometimes dangerously low. When he went to work at this medical clinic, I noticed that there was a complete turnaround. One day, I saw these scribbled letters on a piece of paper on the kitchen table: OCTDM. I asked him, "What do they stand for?" He shrugged, "It has to do with the clinic." I asked, "Is it a medical term?" "No," he explained, "we've got these women at the clinic who come up to me and say, 'Oh, Christopher, you're doing a great job. We really like having you here.'" Now I knew the reason why he felt so much better about his job than he did about school. I still pursued, "Well, but what do the letters stand for?" He shrugged, "They stand for 'old chicks that dig me.'" I laughed and thought, "This kid is going to make it!"

INSIGHT #27

Praise work that's
well done and see
the effect of
appreciation spread
beyond work to
families and
communities.

Oh yes, motivation in the workplace. We can't afford the luxury of having lazy workers stand around. We've got a lot to do! (And if you're going to lean against anything, make sure no one sees you!)

INSIGHT #28

Correct work
that's too slow;
productivity is now a
global competition.

There seems to be an awful lot of whining going on in this world. In fact, there are some people out there who believe this button.

The
more you
complain,
the longer
God lets
you live

INSIGHT #29

If you don't like employment,
try unemployment.
Enforce a
"No Whining" policy
or else risk creating some
very negative teams.

N one of us likes to work with a crab. If people like this are out of the office with a bad cold, everyone back at work is praying they get pneumonia. If they walk out in front of your car, you've got to think about which pedal to push. This sign reminds us to have the right people doing the right thing at the right time with the right attitude.

INSIGHT #30

Get rid of the crabs
in your organization.
(And if you're the crab
and own the business...
well, be careful
when you step out
in front of any cars.)

How many of you feel that you're working with these types of people every day? They certainly are not what you would call "great team players." These are the kinds of people who come to the table to take. They make businesses go bankrupt and customers go crazy.

INSIGHT #31

If you're not sure
whether you have
"leeches" and
"fatheads"
in your organization,
ask the other
team members.

Someone spent a bunch of money building this ball field and certainly doesn't want anyone playing on it! We don't know what this field will be used for, but certainly not for walking around on, let alone maybe bringing a ball to and having some fun. I'm sure someone was probably arrested.

When questionable
rules are set for people
in your organization,
make sure everyone
understands why.

WHAM stands for "we had another meeting." I think many organizations have way too many meetings. I believe that team communication is very important, but it doesn't always take a meeting. When meetings occur, try cutting down their length. Set start and end times, and have a reason for the meeting. Continue to ask the question, "Is this meeting necessary?"

Take away the
chairs and donuts and
meetings go a lot faster!

H ere's one final thought on teamwork and leadership. Do you work for an organization where getting things done is a bit cumbersome? Perhaps you have had a past employer like this. In today's fast-paced world, we just don't have time for an "elephant" approach.

GETTING THINGS DONE AROUND HERE IS LIKE MATING ELEPHANTS

1. It's done at a high level.
2. It's accomplished with a great deal of roaring and screaming.
3. It takes two years to produce results.

INSIGHT #34

Constantly analyze
the process of
how and when
the team members get
their work completed.

CHAPTER 3

QUALITY
IN
BUSINESS

B usinesses could certainly run better if they understood these two phrases. Business owners and managers need to constantly ask, "What have we done today to make sure that our customers feel pleased, or surprised, or special?" Customers will come back if they know they are liked and someone is willing to go beyond what's expected to meet their needs. Businesses also need to figure out what it is that turns customers off. All of us as customers would love to tell a business the reason that we won't come back again or why we're so upset with them. Unfortunately, many businesses aren't interested in listening. Businesses need to understand how much customers can help. An open dialogue can be the basis for a very helpful partnership.

We Impress
Our Customers By...

We Turn Off
Our Customers By...

INSIGHT #35

To increase quality,
keep track of progress
with your customers
each week.

This was in a hotel. I saw the sign after I checked in. I wanted to tell them it turned me off as a customer, but I could tell they wouldn't be very interested in my concern. I didn't sleep a wink. If I saw someone with a cigarette, I was looking around for a garden hose!

INSIGHT #36

A quality-oriented
organization
fixes anything
that could potentially
cause anxiety to its
customers or employees.

Spelling has never been a strong suit of mine but I do recognize when I don't know how to spell something. That's the time to ask someone or to hit spell check on the computer. I hope I would never paint a sign that had the name of my own town spelled wrong. Eau Claire is where I live. I know how to spell that!

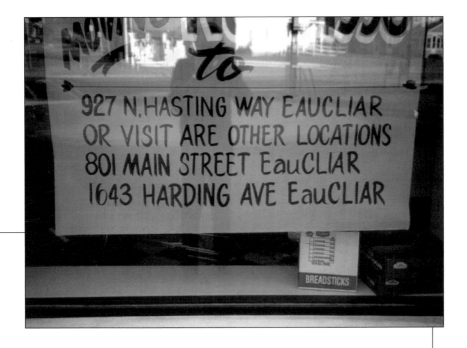

Proof written
communication—
however big or small—
if you plan to project
a quality image.

Ah yes, the politicians have done it again, but this time they've done it with a bit of humor. My hats off to people who are making up the rules in Florida. If you want to breathe dirty air, you know where you can go.

How you
convey rules affects
awareness of and
compliance with them.

This is one of those signs in business that tells workers what they should not be doing. And if one sign doesn't do the job, put up a lot of signs that say the same thing. Of course, everyone responds differently to signs and commands. As you can see, no one's paying too much attention.

INSIGHT #39

If no one believes

the message,

then we don't need the sign.

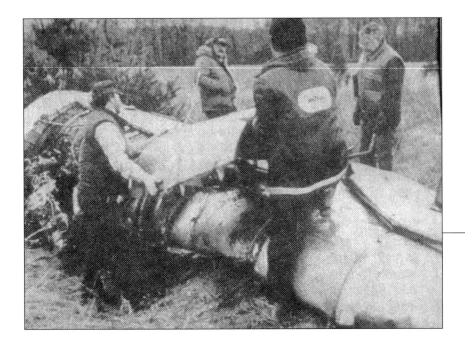

M any times, companies will give the wrong idea to the public. This photo was taken after a plane lost an engine. I don't know about you, but the thought of losing an engine while flying isn't very comforting to me. Note the profound statement by the spokesperson for the airline: "Loss of jet engine extremely rare." My reaction? "Well, I hope so!"

Loss of jet engine: 'Extremely rare'

INSIGHT #40

When making
public statements,
take your customer's
perspective.

This notice is from your government. It is written to a lady who is deceased. It certainly depicts the high efficiency in this governmental office. I'm sure it was the nonthinking computer that wrote this message. I wonder if the recipient called our government for further assistance.

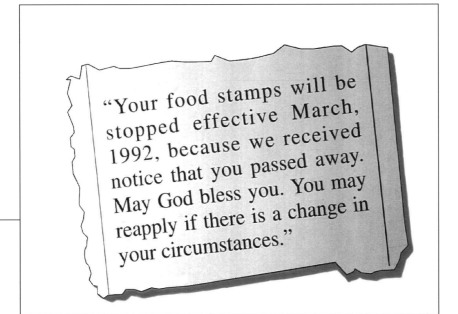

"Your food stamps will be stopped effective March, 1992, because we received notice that you passed away. May God bless you. You may reapply if there is a change in your circumstances."

INSIGHT #41

Think about each
piece of paper that
leaves your office:
Will it make sense
to the recipient and
project a quality image?

found this sign at an auto dealers' state convention. Notice Rule #4. Even car dealers can make fun of themselves.

Best Ball Rules

1. **All players must play the best shot.**

2. **You must use each person's drive twice during the nine holes of play.**

3. **Three Minute Rule applies for lost balls.**

4. **Auto Dealer Ethics apply.**

5. **HAVE FUN!!!!**

INSIGHT #42

If there are no ethics,
you can't have quality.

P eople are always complaining about job evaluation! Hey, this is the ultimate in job evaluation. It happens in a split second.

How would you like a job
where if you made a mistake,
a big red light comes on
and 18,000 people boo?

Jacque Plant
Hockey goalie

INSIGHT #43

Evaluation of
quality is a
minute-by-minute event.

I've always loved this quote by Mae West. What a great philosopher she was. How many times, especially when things are going really well, have we tried to do something to goof it up? Perhaps we don't feel comfortable with the success that we're having so we say to ourselves, "Well, I think failure is just around the corner," and sure enough, there it is! We constantly need to look for success, enjoy success, and repeat success.

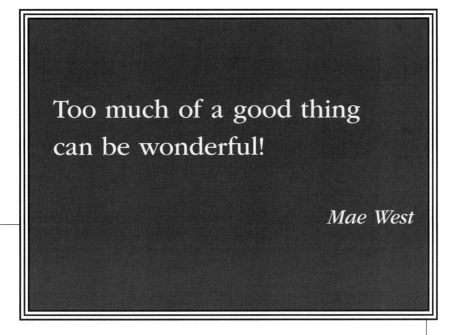

Too much of a good thing can be wonderful!

Mae West

INSIGHT #44

When we stay
focused on quality,
success follows.

Quality in business—and in all of our relationships—can be distilled down to doing the right thing. None of us hates quality. When someone brings us a nice meal, we don't say, "Oh this is much too good for me! Bring me some slop!" No, we eat it and ask for more!

People love quality.

CHAPTER 4

CHANGE AND PROBLEM SOLVING IN BUSINESS

C hange in business surrounds us. Just about the time we think we've figured out the changes that are coming at us, someone presents more changes. We may feel that we are a machine out there, dealing with change. Let me remind you that change was changed before it was changed. Today's status quo was yesterday's change. Change is part of what our life is about. How we handle that change is the key to survival.

> # Change will occur when the pain of change is less than the pain of remaining the same.
>
> *Rayburn Jack*

Rayburn Jack had a great quote. Isn't it true that all of us will change when it's easier to change than to stay where we are?

INSIGHT #46

How change is
presented to others
determines how
they react to it.

People are often stressed out by change. Of course, it's not the change that drives us nuts but our reaction to it. There are three types of "change people"—the adapters, the resisters, and the coasters. The adapters say, "OK, we'll figure out how to make this work." The resisters say, "No way! Why should we make this change?" The coasters say, "Anything you want. It doesn't matter to me. Jump off a building? Sure, I don't care. Another 13 years, I'm out of this place. What difference does it make?" Adapters are the heartbeat of a business. Resisters keep us honest. Not all changes are needed. Coasters will put plywood on our windows. They go out and have a second meeting to undermine the change that everyone else has accepted.

In today's
business world,
there's no room
for coasters.

How many of us have felt that there's only one way to do something? We wonder why we can't keep doing things the way that they have always been done. Well, that is a choice, but I'm not sure it's any less stressful. Consider the businesses that resisted computers years ago, then scrambled to catch up. Even though we're getting good results with the old way, sometimes change will improve the results and make life easier.

INSIGHT #48

When deciding
whether to change,
we need to analyze
the activity involved
and the result
of that activity.

How many times in business are there detours—those little unexpected changes in course—and everyone wonders where they'll end up? Being a little bit upside-down in the new direction is predictable during change situations. Leaders stay calm during these upside-down times and stave off panic in their team members.

nytime we embark on a new path, we're hit by barriers. Persistence is the key.

INSIGHT #49

To get where you want to be,
be persistent
in outlasting detours and
going around barriers.

How's this for a mixed signal? How many times have you read one thing and been told another? Such confusion takes away a lot of energy that could be used more productively. When the direction of change is unclear, the team must stop and agree on the game plan.

INSIGHT #50

Insist on clarification
when the new
direction is unclear.

So often, people believe that they are going through hard times. Actually, these are the easy times for most of us. Being shot at when you leave your house is hard times. No food is hard times. A good share of the world's population spends its waking hours trying to find food. We spend our waking hours trying to work it off.

INSIGHT #51

Keep change
in perspective.
Compare challenges
that you are experiencing
with the bigger problems
in the world.

N ow this is quite a bump. You hit this bump and you'll know it! I especially like the next sign, which provided an editorial comment about how big a bump this really was.

INSIGHT #52

Plan for
unexpected obstacles.
They're predictably present.

've always liked this quote. I think it's important that we continue to struggle. I see people in businesses who feel they have it made, and suddenly they aren't doing as well.

One of the things that helped me have the kind of career I have was that I never reached the point where I thought I had arrived.

Steve Largent
U.S. Representative–Oklahoma

INSIGHT #53

It can take a long time
to recover from the
arrogance of feeling
you no longer
need to improve.

Over the years, I have left a lot of money on the table. As a salesperson (by the way, we're all salespeople), I constantly need to take a look at problems of my customers and ask, "How can I turn these problems around to be revenue-generating for them and for me?" We can all work a little smarter. We need to ask more questions, dig a little deeper into the given situation, and help our customers more.

INSIGHT #54

Look for opportunities
when problems arise.

A nyone who would put up a sign like this in a bathroom is not really helping us solve our problems. When solving problems, we need to understand that we are part of the problem and also part of the solution. We also have to understand that it's essential to look for the root cause of the problem. For too long, I've looked on the surface; now I try to look for why something is happening and why it is continually happening. Perhaps that will help us solve the problems around us.

Anticipate problems.

Search for the cause

of the cause

of the problem.

Businesses need to understand that they're in the solution business. Most of us don't seek out a business unless we have a reason and would like them to be part of the solution to our problems.

WE SELL SOLUTIONS

INSIGHT #56

Offer customers
solutions instead
of problems.

How many times have we felt like this? Underneath that dirt, there's a clean face.

INSIGHT #57

We all have to
wipe the mud off
and start again at times.

There are a lot of things that bug all of us. Maybe frogs have the right idea. My mother always asked, "Who's going to care a hundred years from now?" The answer almost always is, "Nobody."

INSIGHT #58

We can let things
bother us,
change them,
or just ignore them.
When the latter works, do it!

This is one of the first things that I wrote. I wrote it on a piece of scrap paper and you can see the eraser marks as I changed words around. The last line still holds true: Tomorrow is now. Too many of us become soonas people. Soonas the kids leave home, then we'll do something. Soonas we get a little more money, then we'll do something. Soonas I retire, we're gonna buy a motorhome and go to Phoenix. We'll start having fun then. I don't know if you've noticed…you get to be about 64½, you can hardly shift those big buggers!

INSIGHT #59

Make the changes
you've always dreamed
of making now.

CHAPTER 5

EDUCATIONAL
AND
PERSONAL GROWTH
OF TEAM MEMBERS

Announcing the arrival of
Michael Paul
on March 9, 1943 weight 8 lb. 12 oz
Gladys & Paul McKinley

H
ere it is in 1943! Paul and Gladys's little baby boy has arrived! I'll bet they were really proud. Look at the size of this kid.

H ere I am, a little bit older. Pretty cute, don't you think?

INSIGHT #60

We're here because of our parents.
Appreciate what they've taught you.

129

This picture really helps me understand what life is all about. You start in one and end in the other. My father always said, "You come into this world and you have no hair, you have no teeth, you can't walk, you can't talk. You leave this world and…" Guess what? It's exactly the same way. Kind of puts it all in perspective, doesn't it?

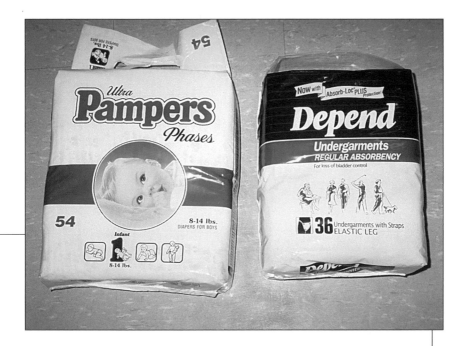

Life is a journey.
Make sure
you're enjoying
the trip both at
work and at home.

WMUD stands for "what makes us different." So many of us believe that being different is wrong. But all of us are striving to be different. Just observe your children.

For a growth-filled life,
as soon as someone
starts figuring you out,
change!

For years, I've built my business on being better and being different, which creates memories. Customers are attracted to businesses that are pleasingly different. Being better and being different require constant learning and growing.

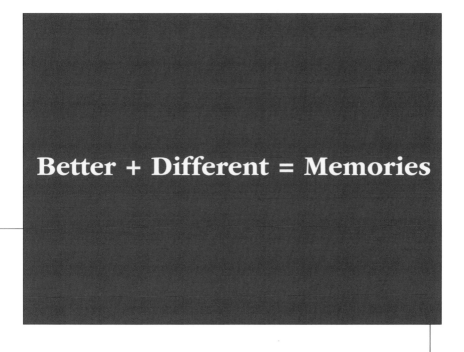

Better + Different = Memories

INSIGHT #63

When customers
remember you,
they'll be back to
spend their money.

This acronym stands for "Mothers Against Dyslexia." Yes, I know some of you are looking at this sign and feeling it looks just fine. Well, I can make fun of this because my wiring is mixed up. I'm dyslexic. I went through high school and college not reading. It was a frustrating time. I could have quit, given my reading disability, but I figured out alternatives. In college, I studied with the smart kids. I took them out for coffee and then asked them questions about classes. I rarely missed a lecture. Now, I listen to tapes. I have tapes everywhere. Tapes in the car, tapes in the office, tapes all over the house. Pretty soon, I'm going to buy a tape player!

D.A.M.

INSIGHT #64

Even with
"mixed-up wiring,"
each of us can
find alternative ways
of learning.

My father always talked about continually learning. Learning is pointless, however, unless implementation occurs. Using what we've learned is what makes for success at work and at home.

INSIGHT #65

If you're not
learning and implementing,
you're going backwards.

Nervous?

They don't know your script.

Paul McKinley

My father observes that you don't have to be nervous, because people don't know your script. (What great advice for salespeople!) He also insists you have to sing your song!

Unless you get up to sing,
they'll never know
you have a song.

Paul McKinley

INSIGHT #66

When implementing
what you've learned,
don't be frightened
about what people
will think of you.

N orm from *Cheers* is one of my great heroes. Talk about philosophers, Norm is right up there with Aristotle, Socrates, and Will Rogers. This is probably my favorite philosophy of the world as seen by Norm.

In this dog-eat-dog world, we're all wearing Milkbone underwear.

Norm
"Cheers"

INSIGHT #67

Always look around
to see who or what
is draining energy from you,
then decide what you're
going to do about it.

Personal growth comes through our own experience and effort. Taking shortcuts and praying can influence growth, too. You can hope all you want, but nothing changes without action.

INSIGHT #68

Grow however and
wherever you can.

All of us need to think about our future, our goals, and how we're going to enjoy the rest of our lives. Even this group was thinking about the future with the theme for their convention. (Think about the implications of that for the rest of us!) Building for tomorrow is all right, but we have to take care of today. Similarly, goals are okay, but I would much rather put my emphasis on the progress that I'm making to reach those goals.

INSIGHT #69

Usually when you
set your goals and
reach them
very quickly,
you haven't set them
high enough.

Today's the day to move forward with your personal growth. If you're procrastinating, volunteer in a long-term health care facility or a hospice program. You'll appreciate the short time each of us is given to pursue our dreams.

INSIGHT #70

Pretend you
have been told
you have a terminal illness
if it motivates you to get going.

CHAPTER 6

BALANCING
WORK AND HOME

There really are a lot of different kinds of relationships out there!

Robin Royster and Dave Elvig began their blissful married life on August 13, 1994 at 1st Baptist Church Of Eau Claire. Rev. Harvey Peters of Madison's Luther Memorial Church presided.

In spite of the picture, they're seriously married!

This couple should be put in a home. They actually put an ad in the paper to advertise their wedding. We need to check their medication.

INSIGHT #71

Keep any relationship
as exciting and unpredictable
as the two participants need.

N ancy picked me up at the airport with this sign. I thought I'd be funny and walk right by. Interestingly enough, someone else walked up to her! I don't know what that was all about.

INSIGHT #72

Take time to
create fun
in your relationships
at work and at home.

What can I say? Each of us needs to answer this question in our own relationships.

When we dig ourselves
into bad spaces in our
relationships, know
how to dig back out—
quickly!

've been around people all my life and not once has anyone ever come up to me and complained, "My partner is just way too romantic. I wish it would stop! I'm sick of it!" Maybe we all need to get more romantic. Nancy and I decided several years ago to go back to going together. Remember "going together"? You'd be thinking all day, "Wheee! We get to be together tonight!" Then you get married and something happens. You hear romantic things like, "WOULD YOU HURRY UP?!" I urge you to go back to going together. It's fun. And get more romantic. If you want to get some spark back into your relationship, bring home a pizza, take off all your clothes, sit in the living room, and eat it. I'll guarantee you, there'll be leftovers!

HOW ROMANTIC CAN YOU GET?

INSIGHT #74

If you're romantic,
you can get
away with anything.
You can leave
your underwear
in the corner for a week
and nobody cares.

159

This has been my motto for many years. In fact, one of the titles of my presentations is "Staying alive...wait until you're dead before you die!" A lot of people walking around are dead. Their bodies just haven't fallen down. Someone says, "Did you hear that Harry died?" and actually, Harry's been dead for 30 years. His body just finally gave out.

Acting dead
while still alive
shortchanges everyone
at work and at home.

I've always thought everyone should wear one of these buttons. Sometimes, a person's fun meter is at an all-time low. Maybe everyone should have one implanted somewhere in their heart. That way, when you saw it was low, you could go up to them and say, "Hey have you heard the latest joke?" or "Let's have some fun. What do you think?"

INSIGHT #76

People who help others laugh
are among the
greatest servants on earth.

When Phil Donahue asked George Burns how he had been able to stay in show business for so long, he observed, "You've got to learn to like what you do for a living." George Burns was in show business for over 90 years! How would you like to be doing the job you're in for 90 years? Maybe you'd like it OK, but could you find the right building?

You've got to learn to like
what you do for a living.

George Burns

INSIGHT #77

The building is not responsible for
our happiness at work.
You and the other people are.

T his is my dentist. I think he skipped a few classes when he was in dental school. I'm a bit frightened of him. Every time I get into his chair at the dental office, he has this funny laugh.

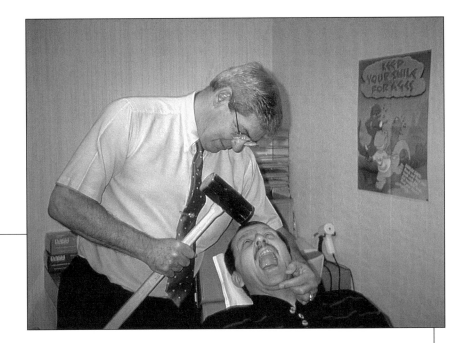

Take what you do seriously,
but not who you are.

These cards came from our daughter while she was in college. I think they're teaching classes in college these days on how to weasel money out of parents. Notice to whom the postcard is addressed. Don't believe it!

Yo DAD!
Guido says $300
By March or
I end up in
the trunk of A
BUICK At the
Bottom of the
MISSISSIPPI —HELP!!
MARY

MICHAEL MCKINLEY
7021 W. LOWES CR. RD
EAU CLAIRE, WI
54701

0 42516 20002 4

INSIGHT #79

Instill a sense of
humor in your children
and you've given
them a lifelong gift.

This is a reality check. So many people just put things off. They don't use the money that they've earned. I came into this world and I owed money to the hospital and the doctor. I'll leave this world and I'll probably owe money again to the hospital, the doctor, and maybe even the funeral home. I asked my 82-year-old uncle what he would do differently if he had his life to live over. As quickly as I could ask, he replied, "I would have spent my money earlier!"

INSIGHT #80

To help balance your life,
weigh out the money you spend
and the money you save.

I grew up in a small town in northern Minnesota. This sign is located there. The family now has several funeral homes and is in its third generation of ownership. The whole time I was growing up, we said, "De Cease Funeral Home is de best!"

INSIGHT #81

You know you're dead
when you get to Cease.
(In the meantime, be alive!)

This sign says it all. You want to lead your life to the fullest because you understand that once you're on this road, it's the last trip you're going to take. So many people never get to ride in a Cadillac until they take this ride. I'd just as soon partake of that experience long before I get here.

INSIGHT #82

Cemetery Road
is a one-way trip.

Placement of these two signs couldn't be better. It certainly has a message for me. Maybe every funeral home should have signs like this next to the building. Ah, but maybe it would be a detriment to sales!

INSIGHT #83

If you don't eat right,
you know where
you might end up...
sooner, not later.

All of us have talents. All of us have just a certain amount of time. The challenge is to use our talents in the available time.

What we do with
what we have
is the key
to a fulfilled life.

Anyone who has ever lived on a farm knows about this sign. People who are farmers have to live with the weather and seem to work night and day. My brother-in-law is a farmer and I have such high respect for him. By the way, he seldom rests.

INSIGHT #85

Get just enough rest
to live life to its fullest
without sleeping away
any extra precious time.

CHAPTER 7

HUMOR AT
WORK AND HOME

This box was in our warehouse for several years, I walked by it hundreds of times before I saw the humor in it. Sometimes humor can be right underneath our noses and we miss it. You see, this is a cardboard box. It's not a plastic box. It's not a metal box. It's a cardboard box. Someone put the sign on the side to make sure that we remembered.

INSIGHT #86

The most familiar
sights around us
can also be the funniest,
if we stop to notice.

George Burns has many, many great quotes. I have this one on the wall in my office. I read it almost everyday that I'm there. I know that George will be remembered for a long time.

There's not a thing I do now
that I didn't do when I was 18,
which shows you
how pathetic I was at 18.

Comedian George Burns
on what he's like at 98

INSIGHT #87

People who can
laugh at themselves
are the most fun to be with,
whatever age they might be.

When your business comes down to wearing signs like these, you know you're in trouble. But the second sign depicts that I'm a man of the nineties. I'm watching my weight. I'm eating healthy food.

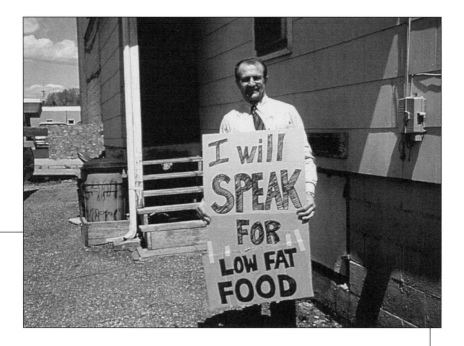

People who can laugh
at the business they're in
enjoy work the most.

This button needs no explanation!

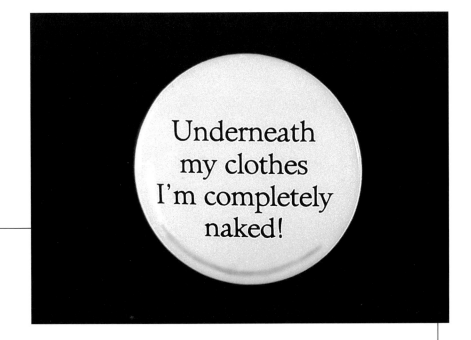

INSIGHT #89

When you think
there's nothing to laugh at,
do what I do:
Take all your clothes off
and stand in front of the mirror.
(You'll get a chuckle. Okay,
maybe not as big a chuckle
as I get!)

191

Quote of the Day

A dance studio in Manhattan is offering all nude men's dance classes. Besides the advantage of saving tons on outfits, owner **Robert Yahn** said:

S ome people make the darnedest quotes. I don't think I'd want to watch.

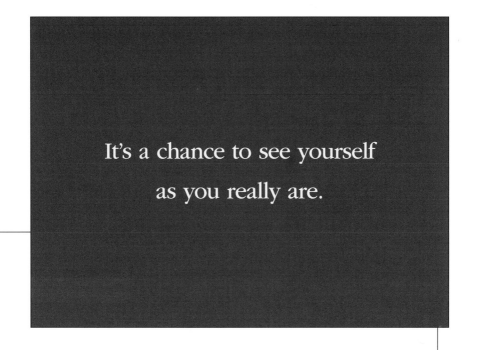

It's a chance to see yourself

as you really are.

INSIGHT #90

If you don't think
"seeing yourself as you really are"
is funny, you haven't tried
standing in front
of the mirror yet.

I saw this sign near a convention at which I was speaking. I thought this group must be really desperate if they have an area where you can talk about these types of things. I went over there and wanted to join the organization, but they wouldn't let me.

s this any way to advertise for business? I hope this hotel is near the "Convention Affairs" people!

INSIGHT #91

The best affair you can
have is with laughter.

Most people would read this particular ad and not laugh at all. I thought, "This is quite a truck!" I called. It had already been sold!

1979 GMC 4-speed 4x4, lock outs, clean 4-way Meyer plow. $2,450. Also—tilt 14' trailer with duals & wench. $750. Eau Claire.

INSIGHT #92

Read the newspaper
for humor.

I saw this sign in an airport. If this is the last shuttle that's going out, I don't want to get on!

Read the signs
around you
for humor.

Can you imagine the number of people who have driven by these signs and never really gotten the second meaning? I've often wondered what the workers in the county crew who posted the signs were thinking. My guess is they probably didn't have a clue what they had done.

INSIGHT #94

When you look backwards,
you can often see
the humor that
previously eluded you.

T his sign not only offers a warning, but a threat. Perhaps in the time it takes you to read the sign, the bull would be upon you! Can you see someone out in the pasture with a stopwatch, clocking how fast the bull could run? Can't you hear someone say, "Ah, honey, come on. Let's make a run for it!"

Sometimes the best
way to get an
important message across
is to make people laugh.

When I read this sign, I thought this has to be the golf course for me. I'm one of the slowest golfers out there.

Then I got worried. I found this sign. Maybe they put it up to slow us golfers down so they could get a better bead on us.

INSIGHT #96

Watch for opportunities
to add humor to the
world around you.

found these two signs within minutes from one another. They were in a neighborhood that had very creative people. Both of these signs are warnings that invite you to take a second glance and chuckle a bit. I sat around the "Amorous Duck" sign for two hours. Nothing happened.

INSIGHT #97

Creativity
sets in when we
find humorous ways
to communicate
a message.

A woman who worked in a nursing home gave me this button. Some days, I look in the mirror and say, "Hmmm, I can't remember where I'm supposed to go." I'm writing a lot of lists now, except I keep forgetting where I put my lists.

INSIGHT #98

We can either
laugh or cry about
our memory lapses.
I'd rather laugh.

Look...a flowerbed. Do you know how many people drove by this scene and never really got it? How about the person who painted this bed, put dirt in it, and planted flowers? Wouldn't you like to meet this person? This person has a very exciting sense of humor. I would guess the individual who did this is quite a character.

INSIGHT #99

Life is not boring
when you surround
yourself with
fun "characters."

I see a lot of people who get to about 4:00 in the afternoon and aren't interested in doing anything but grabbing some sleep. George Burns believed that you were getting older when the swimsuit issue of *Sports Illustrated* came out and you were upset because there were too many pictures and not enough articles. I like getting older. A lot of people are all upset because they're having another birthday. I like having birthdays. NOT having birthdays doesn't excite me. When you stop having birthdays, it's over. At my age, I celebrate my birthday for a whole week. I know I'm not going to get many more.

Smile a lot.

People will wonder

what you're up to!

LIST OF INSIGHTS

Insight #1: Know your mission at work.

Insight #2: Provide special service and customers will feel good about paying more...then coming back again.

Insight #3: If you forgo convenience, customers won't feel good about paying more.

Insight #4: Focus on appreciation, the backbone of customer loyalty.

Insight #5: Believe people will buy, ask them, and some will.

Insight #6: Make it easy for customers to do business with you.

Insight #7: Consider the relationship between your business and the weather from your customer's perspective. (Most customers expect you to provide service no matter what.)

Insight #8: Customers interpret our signs any way they want to.

Insight #9: Beware that oxymorons can be fun—or confusing— for your customers.

Insight #10: Listen to your customers; they'll tell you what you should be selling.

Insight #11: Provide only positive messages when people come to your place of business.

Insight #12: Businesses can attract (or deter) customers with their name.

Insight #13: Marketing plans come in many different sizes and colors.

Insight #14: Diversify in a way that makes sense to your customers.

Insight #15: Indulge customers with free "stuff" whenever you can.

Insight #16: It's OK to let your customers know what's fair to take for free and what's not.

Insight #17: Let your customers know what you need and expect from them.

Insight #18: Do what you can to make shopping with children a pleasant experience; it will keep the adults coming back.

Insight #19: Make spending money with your business fun!

Insight #20: Take care of your business...or someone else will!

Insight #21: Build strong teams if you want a strong organization.

Insight #22: If each of us would individually commit to being firm, fair, flexible, and fun, we'd build incredibly strong teams at work (and at home).

Insight #23: The "fun" part of teamwork is important to model; be able to laugh at yourself.

Insight #24: Everybody has days when they say, "Boy, today was a laugher!"…and, long-term, the work still gets done.

Insight #25: The smartest leaders and the strongest teams have often made the most mistakes in the past.

Insight #26: Guide people toward a common goal and they'll know who the leader is.

Insight #27: Praise work that's well done and see the effect of appreciation spread beyond work to families and communities.

Insight #28: Correct work that's too slow; productivity is now a global competition.

Insight #29: If you don't like employment, try unemployment. Enforce a "No Whining" policy or else risk creating some very negative teams.

Insight #30: Get rid of the crabs in your organization. (And if you're the crab and own the business…well, be careful when you step out in front of any cars.)

Insight #31: If you're not sure whether you have "leeches" and "fatheads" in your organization, ask the other team members.

Insight #32: When questionable rules are set for people in your organization, make sure everyone understands why.

Insight #33: Take away the chairs and donuts and meetings go a lot faster!

Insight #34: Constantly analyze the process of how and when the team members get their work completed.

Insight #35: To increase quality, keep track of progress with your customers each week.

Insight #36: A quality-oriented organization fixes anything that could potentially cause anxiety to its customers or employees.

Insight #37: Proof written communication—however big or small—if you plan to project a quality image.

Insight #38: How you convey rules affects awareness of and compliance with them.

Insight #39: If no one believes the message, then we don't need the sign.

Insight #40: When making public statements, take your customer's perspective.

Insight #41: Think about each piece of paper that leaves your office: Will it make sense to the recipient and project a quality image?

Insight #42: If there are no ethics, you can't have quality.

Insight #43: Evaluation of quality is a minute-by-minute event.

Insight #44: When we stay focused on quality, success follows.

Insight #45: People love quality.

Insight #46: How change is presented to others determines how they react to it.

Insight #47: In today's business world, there's no room for coasters.

Insight #48: When deciding whether to change, we need to analyze the activity involved and the result of that activity.

Insight #49: To get where you want to be, be persistent in outlasting detours and going around barriers.

Insight #50: Insist on clarification when the new direction is unclear.

Insight #51: Keep change in perspective. Compare challenges that you are experiencing with the bigger problems in the world.

Insight #52: Plan for unexpected obstacles. They're predictably present.

Insight #53: It can take a long time to recover from the arrogance of feeling you no longer need to improve.

Insight #54: Look for opportunities when problems arise.

Insight #55: Anticipate problems. Search for the cause of the cause of the problem.

Insight #56: Offer customers solutions instead of problems.

Insight #57: We all have to wipe the mud off and start again at times.

Insight #58: We can let things bother us, change them, or just ignore them. When the latter works, do it!

Insight #59: Make the changes you've always dreamed of making now.

Insight #60: We're here because of our parents. Appreciate what they've taught you.

Insight #61: Life is a journey. Make sure you're enjoying the trip both at work and at home.

Insight #62: For a growth-filled life, as soon as someone starts figuring you out, change!

Insight #63: When customers remember you, they'll be back to spend their money.

Insight #64: Even with "mixed-up wiring," each of us can find alternative ways of learning.

Insight #65: If you're not learning and implementing, you're going backwards.

Insight #66: When implementing what you've learned, don't be frightened about what people will think of you.

Insight #67: Always look around to see who or what is draining energy from you, then decide what you're going to do about it.

Insight #68: Grow however and wherever you can.

Insight #69: Usually when you set your goals and reach them very quickly, you haven't set them high enough.

Insight #70: Pretend you have been told you have a terminal illness if it motivates you to get going.

Insight #71: Keep any relationship as exciting and unpredictable as the two participants need.

Insight #72: Take time to create fun in your relationships at work and at home.

Insight #73: When we dig ourselves into bad spaces in our relationships, know how to dig back out—quickly!

Insight #74: If you're romantic, you can get away with anything. You can leave your underwear in the corner for a week and nobody cares.

Insight #75: Acting dead while still alive shortchanges everyone at work and at home.

Insight #76: People who help others laugh are among the greatest servants on earth.

Insight #77: The building is not responsible for our happiness at work. You and the other people are.

Insight #78: Take what you do seriously, but not who you are.

Insight #79: Instill a sense of humor in your children and you've given them a lifelong gift.

Insight #80: To help balance your life, weigh out the money you spend and the money you save.

Insight #81: You know you're dead when you get to Cease. (In the meantime, be alive!)

Insight #82: Cemetery Road is a one-way trip.

Insight #83: If you don't eat right, you know where you might end up…sooner, not later.

Insight #84: What we do with what we have is the key to a fulfilled life.

Insight #85: Get just enough rest to live life to its fullest without sleeping away any extra precious time.

Insight #86: The most familiar sights around us can also be the funniest, if we stop to notice.

Insight #87: People who can laugh at themselves are the most fun to be with, whatever age they might be.

Insight #88: People who can laugh at the business they're in enjoy work the most.

Insight #89: When you think there's nothing to laugh at, do what I do: Take all your clothes off and stand in front of the mirror. (You'll get a chuckle...)

Insight #90: If you don't think "seeing yourself as you really are" is funny, you haven't tried standing in front of the mirror yet.

Insight #91: The best affair you can have is with laughter.

Insight #92: Read the newspaper for humor.

Insight #93: Read the signs around you for humor.

Insight #94: When you look backwards, you can often see the humor that previously eluded you.

Insight #95: Sometimes the best way to get an important message across is to make people laugh.

Insight #96: Watch for opportunities to add humor to the world around you.

Insight #97: Creativity sets in when we find humorous ways to communicate a message.

Insight #98: We can either laugh or cry about our memory lapses. I'd rather laugh.

Insight #99: Life is not boring when you surround yourself with fun "characters."

Insight #100: Smile a lot. People will wonder what you're up to!